# the colorful garden

# the colorful garden

## Creative Planting for Glorious Effects

## RICHARD ROSENFELD

LORENZ BOOKS

First published by Lorenz books in 2001
© Anness Publishing Limited 2001

Lorenz Books is an imprint of
Anness Publishing Limited, Hermes House,
88–89 Blackfriars Road, London SE1 8HA

www.lorenzbooks.com

Published in the USA by
Lorenz Books, Anness Publishing Inc.,
27 West 20th Street, New York NY10011

Distributed in Canada by
Raincoast Books, 9050 Shaunessy Street,
Vancouver, British Columbia V6P 6ES

A CIP catalogue record for this book is available
from the British Library

10 9 8 7 6 5 4 3 2

Publisher **Joanna Lorenz**
Managing Editor **Judith Simons**
Project Editor **Claire Folkard**
Editorial Reader **Jonathan Marshall**
Designer **Mark Latter**
Photographers **Peter Anderson, Jonathan
Buckley, Michelle Garrett, Simon McBride,
Marie O'Hara, Debbie Patterson,
Jo Whitworth**
Stylists **Michelle Garrett, Gilly Love**
Production Controller **Don Campaniello**

# contents

# introduction

The whole point of having a garden is that you completely pack it with colour. But how? If you paint a picture you can immediately check the results. The bizarre thing about gardening is that you invariably have to wait until the following year to see if a scheme actually works. The purpose of rearranging and rejigging the plants in the garden is to find out which plants "make the leap and crackle and blend", as Monet said, and prove they are as good as everyone says and give you a terrific result.

The most exciting part of creating a brand new colour scheme is that rare, random event that upgrades it from being really smart to being absolutely sensational. You've crammed the earth with bulbs, hundreds of tiny horticultural underground time bombs waiting to ping up and flower, and perennials that bloom in the most amazing, well-organized sequence, then something quite astonishing happens, and a giant sunflower self-seeds in the salvias and you realize what was missing all along.

But you can only achieve that extra, magical tweak if you are already 99 per cent on the right track. This book explains it all. It shows you how to combine colours creatively. Then it's up to you.

# how colour works in the garden

The first big rule about using colour in the garden is anything goes. And second, there are some clever tricks, and the best of them go like this.

You can make a garden seem longer by putting pale colours at the far end, so the space seems to filter away. And you get the opposite effect by using strong colours which bring everything right in and much closer. They hint at different dimensions. If you want to create eye-catchers, to get people to look more here than there, use snappy adjuncts like red and yellow, or blue and orange which grab the eye. But be

**BELOW** *Dahlia* 'Aylett's Gaiety' works well underplanted with rich blue forget-me-nots and grape hyacinths.

careful. Such combinations or clashes mean you can't plant a subtle pastel beauty nearby because it won't get a look in. It'll be dwarfed, diminished, and blotted out. Instead, make it the star of its own special, quiet arrangement. All gardens need quiet areas, a kind of tension-free hum before you get on to the trumpets.

## Lighting

Try to place some star plants where they will be lit by the sun. *Molinia caerulea arundinacea* is a terrific grass that grows quite large, with a mound of 90cm (3ft) high leaves and flowering stems poking 1.5m (5ft) higher. It glows a fierce sugary-orange in the middle of autumn – electric, alive and luminous. If you can't find it, 'Zuneigung' is even better, like a porcupine on fire. It's one plant you don't hide away in the gloom. Make sure you plant it in a big open space where it can be seen lit by the orange-gold autumn sun. The same applies to anything red (dahlias, or roses in fire-engine red such as 'Parkdirektor Riggers', which really pick up this glow), orange (kniphofias), and yellow (the flashy foliage of a liquidambar before it falls).

If you like growing cannas, go for 'Durban', with its striped foliage. They look terribly dull with the sun shining full on them, all pink and black stripes without any life at all, but when the sun is shining through the foliage they look 1,000 per cent better, shot with orange and green. You've also got to think about placing yellow. Back-lit yellow, with the sun shining through from behind, like through a stained glass window, is nothing like yellow with the sun blasting full frontal. The effects are totally different.

And that is one of the big points about colour. It is not fixed. For example, distance creates different tones. When you look at a red close up it has plenty of clout, but seen further away the effect is calmer, and not so "in your face".

If you place pink under a fierce overhead sun it looks washed out, but at dusk and dawn it is darker. So is pale blue. In fact if you want a blue garden, the time of day when it really stands out is early evening. That is because the eye is better at picking up blue in fading light, the very time when the light has a blue cast, which gets reflected back by anything blue. All of which means if you want blues to stand out, plant them in semi-shade. And if white is your favourite colour, it is far better at twilight when it leaps out of the growing dark than at midday when it is rather harsh.

## Colour Combinations

Think of gardening as flower arranging on a big scale and you'll quickly see how it works. Nothing is grown in isolation. You can use blocks of colour like blue forget-me-nots (*Myosotis sylvatica*) with yellow tulips such as 'West Point', and both colours stand out that bit more. The technique works extremely well with blue and orange, and yellow and purple. You can also use blocks of

BELOW Green is valid as a colour in its own right as this lavish planting scheme shows.

ABOVE **A fresh spring bulb display of 'Heart's Delight'
tulips interplanted with** *Chionodoxa luciliae*

colour like purple around a few whites,
and they elbow their neighbours upstage.

You can even combine two colours to hint at
an illusory third. Red and yellow give the ghost of
an orange, and blues with reds suggest purple.

## Repeat Planting

You need a big garden and plenty of space to
indulge in blocks of one colour. One trick is
well worth copying. If you pack together various
blues such as 'Perle d'Azur', the bluest clematis,
and *Cerinthe major* 'Purpurascens', you
inevitably look closer and closer, studying the
nuances, texture and shapes. The monochrome
draws you in.

You can also use repeat plantings of certain
colours in borders to make the eye skip along.

Start with groups of three, then seven, nine, and
thirteen, and you build up a lively rhythm. You
can also use this technique to avoid creating a
garden with big, bold, separate blotches of
colour. Group most of your whites together, but
make sure you get scatterings of white all
around to help the eye move on.

## Reflections

One of the main advantages of a big garden
pond is that it can catch big reflections, muted
but strong. The best you can get are the
powerful reds and yellows when the foliage on
Japanese maples (*Acer palmatum*), spindle trees
(*Euonymus*) and tupelos (*Nyssa*) fire up their
autumn show. You double the colours on offer.

## Classic Combinations and Surprises

Nobody plants a garden in one go. Start with
what's on sale now, then decide which colour
goes best next to each plant. That's the easy
bit. But if you need a white, which white?
*Crambe cordifolia*, with its floaty aerial haze of
tiny white flowers? Or a knee-high
*Argyranthemum* with white daisy-like flowers? Or
the great whoosh of scented white flowers on
common jasmine (*Jasminum officinale*)? You
choose. That's the first stage.

The second is getting extra colours to pop up
in every season. And the third stage involves
mixing colour with size, shape and texture, the
best example being one of the best sights in any
garden – a late spring to early summer laburnum
tunnel. The longer the tunnel the better, with

thousands of bright yellow flowers hanging down, above your head, and stabbing out of the ground drumstick purple alliums giving bright colours, thin verticals, balls, and an absolutely astonishing mass of droopy, dangly flowers.

## Extra Kinds of Colour

Flowers are the big starting point when thinking up a colour scheme, but they are not the end of the story. Coloured stems and berries are incredibly important, especially when winter zaps many flowers. The range is surprisingly large. If you want smart, brilliant coloured stems, *Acer palmatum* 'Sango-kaku' is the one for red. Add the effect of the dogwoods, like the red-stemmed *Cornus alba* 'Sibirica', and *Tilia platyphyllos* 'Rubra' limes which have a fuzz of red twigs high on top of the tree, then all you need is snow to really bring out the colours.

The best berry-bearing plants include *Callicarpa bodinieri* 'Profusion' with hundreds of tiny, shiny, lilac balls on bare winter branches, reaching about 3m (10ft) high. Grow it near *Clematis* 'Bill Mackenzie', which produces wonderful, silvery spidery seedheads when the yellow flowers are dead. For the biggest, fattest berries on a rose, get 'Scabrosa', which makes a great flowering bush with a profusion of crimson-pink blooms. *Rosa macrophylla* 'Master Hugh' has monster hips. And if you want hips high up, dangling out of trees, try *Rosa helenae*, 5.4m (18ft) high, which runs heads of white flowers through trees.

Then there are hollies (*Ilex*) and the rare *Ilex ketambensis* with 2.5cm- (1in-) long berries. And firethorn (*Pyracantha*), *Sorbus*, and *Viburnum davidii* with its gorgeous turquoise egg-shaped berries (you'll need male and female plants to get them). And if you want bright, fat, fleshy, succulent berries to attract birds, you will need to grow cotoneaster for sparrows, starlings and thrushes, hawthorn (*Crataegus*) for blue tits, finches and pheasants, and holly for bullfinches, robins and waxwings. Garden colour is good for us, and it attracts the wildlife.

**BELOW A beautiful display that is easy on the eye, using purple sage, euphorbia, lavender and irises.**

# yellow

Yellow is one of the key garden colours. You can use it in great clusters in spring with daffodils (*Narcissus*) and crocuses, out on the lawn and under deciduous trees, and to jazz up the dull days of winter with mahonias and winter jasmine (*Jasminum nudiflorum*).

The value of yellow used in small groups with reds or blues is that it immediately grabs the eye. This is especially the case with mulleins such as *Verbascum olympicum*, with its startling spires of flowers. You can use bright yellow in bigger groups, but because it can be overpowering on its own, be sure to include some muted tones. The range of yellow flowers is vast - from lilies that look like hummingbirds to anemones like flashes of butter. Just make sure you choose some with style.

*Lilium* 'Cover Girl'

# bright yellow

Strong yellows make striking look-at-me schemes. If you need
a really dominant shrub try *Berberis* 'Goldilocks', or if you want
a yellow perennial to keep the border alive and kicking into
early autumn, the brilliant deep golden yellow flowers of the
rudbeckias are perfect. And there is a wide range of dahlias,
lilies and roses with incredible shape and style.

ABOVE **Cactus dahlias, such as
'Hidalgo Climax' give a bright, punchy
look to the late summer garden.**

ABOVE **Yarrow (*Achillea*) is indispensable in cottage and wildlife gardens,
here forming drifts of vivid yellow.**

ABOVE **Even small daffodils such as
*Narcissus* 'Rip van Winkle', 13cm
(5in) high, give a colourful show.**

ABOVE **Black-eyed Susan (*Rudbeckia
fulgida* var. *deamii*) gives a flash of
yellow for a strong autumn show.**

ABOVE *Rosa* **'Poulgan' makes an
excellent patio rose for planting in
gaps between paving on a terrace.**

ABOVE **Lilies are never disappointing;
this smart bright yellow will give a
big boost to any midsummer display.**

ABOVE **For a brilliant mid-spring
show of golden daffodils try
*Narcissus* 'Dutch Master'.**

ABOVE *Halimium* x *pauanum* is an evergreen shrub, just right for the front of the early summer border.

ABOVE *Berberis* 'Goldilocks' gives a big display of tiny yellow flowers in spring, followed by dark blue fruit.

ABOVE *Tulipa kolpakowskiana* is a lovely mini tulip, 20cm (8in) high, for the rock garden or front of a border.

ABOVE *Rhododendron luteum* is really a deciduous azalea with a rich scent in late spring and early summer.

ABOVE Daffodils start flowering quite early, and *Narcissus* 'February Gold' is one of the first to bloom.

ABOVE *Iris danfordiae* is a gorgeous, tiny yellow gem, 15cm (6in) high, which flowers in early spring.

ABOVE The monkey flower (*Mimulus*) comes in plenty of smart bright colours such as this vivid yellow.

ABOVE End spring on a high with *Tulipa* 'Hamilton', which has wonderful fringed edges.

ABOVE *Anemone ranunculoides* 'Pleniflora' is a spreading perennial, which bursts into flower in spring.

# spring yellow

**This is the colour to save for spring**. Use it in the biggest boldest groups of daffodils because the great absence of other colours, except green, means it rarely produces clashes. And as the first major colour of spring, it also has wonderful shock value – after days of nothing, suddenly the garden looks like it has been doused in egg yolks. In summer, bright punchy yellows such as *Coreopsis grandiflora* or *Rudbeckia fulgida* 'Goldsturm' will brighten any slightly dull scheme.

BELOW LEFT **The classic late spring mix of vivid, yellow tulips and dark blue forget-me-nots (***Myosotis***).**

BELOW RIGHT *Lysimachia punctata* **gives a strong show from midsummer onwards.**

RIGHT **Daffodils always offer a superb display of spring colour, whether in a border or in grass.**

# pale yellow

Pale yellow is a highly valuable colour that adds to mellow background drifts. It is also a terrific link colour because it blends with green. Try primroses (*Primula*) and wallflowers (*Erysimum cheiri*) in spring, then enjoy honeysuckle (*Lonicera*), daylilies (*Hemerocallis*), and roses in summer. For winter, *Cornus stolonifera* 'Flaviramea' has bendy, watery-yellow shoots.

ABOVE *Dahlia* 'Clair de Lune' is a gentle pale yellow, a good contrast to stronger colours.

ABOVE *Rosa xanthina* 'Canary Bird' is a beautiful spring-flowering shrub, 3m (10ft) high and wide.

ABOVE The soft, pale yellow marigold *Tagetes* 'French Vanilla' likes a hot sunny place in the garden.

ABOVE *Osteospermum* 'Buttermilk' gives beautiful, pale yellow, daisy-like flowers all summer long.

ABOVE A big display of yellow-centred *Dahlia* 'Lilliput' makes a burst of fresh summer colour.

ABOVE *Rosa* 'Peace' is a classic rose, with soft yellow flowers and dark green, glossy leaves.

ABOVE Lilies, especially when they look this good, are key plants in any formal or cottage garden scheme.

ABOVE *Hypericum olympicum* makes a neat 30cm (12in) mound covered with star-shaped flowers.

ABOVE *Rhododendron* 'Narcissiflorum' is a good choice for a medium size garden, with scented spring flowers.

ABOVE Primroses (*Primula*) are perfect in spring, but make sure they get some shade and moist soil.

ABOVE The Chinese *Iris forrestii* blooms in early summer, and has the most exquisite flowers.

ABOVE 'Arthur Bell' is a 90cm (3ft) high, scented rose that keeps flowering all summer long.

ABOVE *Dahlia* 'Lemon Elegans' is a small semi-cactus type, absolutely essential for late summer-autumn.

ABOVE The Alpine bottlebrush (*Callistemon sieberi*) needs a sunny sheltered site.

ABOVE The daylily *Hemerocallis* 'Wind Song' produces prolific, gorgeous, creamy-yellow flowers.

ABOVE *Anthemis tinctoria* 'E.C. Buxton', with its mass of pale yellow flowers, is ideal for a free-flowing scheme.

# soft yellow

**Gardens need surprises, and yellows make a big**
one, especially when you find an unexpected self-enclosed area with
unobtrusive colours mixed with a few jumping-out, brasher tones.
The plants that have the greatest pale yellow presence include spring
tulips, particularly when planted in a huge romping mass, beautiful soft-
toned roses, and best of all, mulleins (*Verbascum*). The tallest ones tend
to be sulphur yellow and their fun, mad spires can hit 1.8m (6ft) by
midsummer. You need at least one of them such as *Verbascum
olympicum* with the far quieter, gentler 'Gainsborough', to give the
scheme a bit of muscle.

FAR LEFT Mulleins, such
as this *Verbascum*
'Gainsborough', are
top-choice plants.

ABOVE LEFT Highlight
pale yellow roses
against an attractive
ornamental feature.

ABOVE RIGHT A frothy
spring display of white
tulips ('Snowpeak' and
'Sweet Harmony') and
mixed wallflowers.

# orange

Colours don't come any hotter than orange, which is why it needs to be used judiciously. Include it in a strong, dominant hothouse display with plenty of reds and yellows, with no attempt to tone it down, or in brief occasional flashes, giving a good surprise.

One of the best oranges is *Crocosmia* 'Emily McKenzie', or *Crocosmia* 'Firebird' with a dash of red. The leaves are like thin, vertical swords, and you can plant them to flash out of shrubs like Mexican orange blossom (*Choisya ternata*). If orange sounds too intense and garish for summer, in winter it is an absolute boon, and there are plenty of excellent shrubs and trees with lashings of orange fruit and berries, such as sorbus, cotoneaster and firethorn (*Pyracantha*). The harder the berries, the less likely the birds are to eat them.

*Hamamelis* 'Jelena'

# warm orange

Orange can be used carefully to lead up to a major show of hothouse reds, or as the dominant colour and the centre of it's own vivid scheme. The flowers with the best colours tend to appear and peak in summer and autumn, and using the latter means you can certainly create end-of-season displays with plenty of marvellous clout. Always go out on a high.

ABOVE There are many annual and perennial marigolds (*Tagetes*) that enliven front of the border displays.

ABOVE Osteospermums typically have white flowers, so when you see an orange one, snap it up.

ABOVE *Rosa* 'Sweet Magic' produces large clusters of orange flowers from early summer to the autumn.

ABOVE *Rhododendron* 'Redshank' gives a deep warm colour. If you don't have acid soil, grow it in a tub.

ABOVE *Lilium davidii* can have up to 40 striking orange-red flowers on each stem, set against dark leaves.

ABOVE *Helianthemum nummularium* is a dwarf spreading shrub, making good ground cover in bright sun.

ABOVE Lion's ear (*Leonotis leonurus*) is a tender South African plant that must be brought indoors over winter.

ABOVE Dahlias are essential in any strong, vivid display, and this orange will hold its own in any group.

ABOVE 'Ellen Huston' is a prize-winning dwarf dahlia with dark foliage that does not need staking.

ABOVE The magnificent water-lily tulip (*Tulipa kaufmanniana*) and its hybrids appear in early spring.

ABOVE *Rosa* 'Warm Welcome' is a new miniature climber reaching 2.1m (7ft) high, with a mass of flowers.

ABOVE The orange daisy-like flowers of *Helenium* 'Chipperfield Orange' are ideal in hot sunny borders.

ABOVE 'Anna Ford', with its orange-red flowers and gold stamens, is a medium size rose, 1.5m (5ft) high.

ABOVE Cannas are the champions of any sub-tropical display, with big leaves and gladioli-like flowers.

ABOVE Poppies (*Papaver*) are easily grown plants that readily self-seed their way around the garden.

ABOVE *Rosa* 'Top Marks' is an exquisite miniature rose ideal for growing by patios.

# brilliant orange

**Orange is one of the brightest garden colours.** If it is used in huge blocks the result can be excessive, so save it for sudden highlights. Make it really stand out by using it against a background of green foliage, especially a dark green hedge of yew (*Taxus*) or beech (*Fagus*). It also makes a lively climax to a yellow-and-red display, and since plants such as dahlias and nasturtiums (*Tropaeolum*) flower plentifully in these colours right though to the end of summer and into autumn, they guarantee the gardening year ends on a high note. If you want it to end even more spectacularly, acquire the red-hot poker *Kniphofia uvaria* 'Nobilis', which stands out like an electrifying lamppost in the border.

warm and **welcoming**
bright **fiery** oranges

RIGHT Flashy hothouse plants like *Crocosmia* 'Lucifer' and *Helenium* 'Waldtraut' always look best in early autumn when they're intensified by the orange cast of the sun.

FAR RIGHT TOP A terrific effect can be achieved with ordinary plants, as with these orange wallflowers and 'Queen of Night' tulips.

FAR RIGHT BOTTOM Flamboyant cannas come in all shapes and sizes, with a few special ones that you can even grow in water.

# red

Red is the key garden colour with real impact. It immediately grabs the eye, but if it is used in large numbers of plants in small gardens, it dominates and blots out everything else. Using it with other colours, especially dotted among whites, yellows, pinks and blues, creates quite beautiful contrasts. Plenty of plants offer superb reds, from hybrid tea or large-flowered bush roses that have tightly scrolled buds (climbing 'Crimson Glory' is one of the best with a gorgeous scent) to annual poppies (*Papaver*), dahlias such as 'Hillcrest Royal', and perennials such as *Potentilla atrosanguinea* 'Gibson's Scarlet'. Plenty of plants also offer dark plum-red foliage such as *Lobelia* 'Queen Victoria'. In big numbers they get a bit gloomy, so use them as a surprise among brighter flowers.

*Rosa* 'Papa Meilland'

# rich red

The reds come in a surprisingly large range, from deep dark maroon to the 'in-your-face' flashy. Choosing the right background is extremely important if their effect is not to be lost. White walls in the case of climbers, and greens and whites for shrubs and perennials, are almost as important as the plants themselves.

ABOVE **For an early spring red the tiny** *Tulipa linifolia* **offers an excellent display of colour.**

ABOVE **Try swirling red ribbons of colour through a border using** *Dahlia* **'Harvest Red Dwarf'**

ABOVE **The new American dahlia 'Tally Ho' is a punchy dark red, excellent in vivid colour schemes.**

ABOVE **The fantastic scarlet** *Passiflora coccinea* **will thrive in a warm conservatory.**

ABOVE **'Ena Harkness' is a climbing midsummer rose that rarely grows more than 4.5m (15ft) high.**

ABOVE *Pelargonium* **'Happy Thought' is a terrific pot plant with crimson flowers and yellow-splashed leaves.**

ABOVE **The most indispensable dahlia is the bright red 'Bishop of Llandaff', with contrasting dark red foliage.**

ABOVE *Rhododendron* 'James Gable' makes a great feature with its show of red flowers in the spring.

ABOVE *Rosa* 'Mister Lincoln' makes an excellent rich red for the border, and provides scores of cut flowers.

ABOVE Verbenas are essential in any display of annuals; they also come in whites, blues, mauves and pinks.

ABOVE *Camellia* 'Bob's Tinsie' is a smart, compact shrub that is covered with brilliant red flowers.

ABOVE Busy Lizzies (*Impatiens*) offer amazing colour all summer, and are just what you need to fill any gaps.

ABOVE *Dahlia* 'Willo's Surprise' has pompom-shaped wine-red flowers that grow about 90cm (3ft) high.

ABOVE *Rosa* 'Dublin Bay' is a mini climber offering shiny dark green leaves and glowing red flowers.

ABOVE 'Bob Hope' is the ideal compact camellia. Its dark red flowers go well with any bright yellow.

ABOVE For late summer to autumn hothouse schemes, you need the likes of this *Dahlia* 'Fire Mountain'.

ABOVE Tulips come in all colours from white to pink and blue, and include some startling reds.

LEFT Bright pot plants like *Pelargonium* 'Harvard' can be used on patios or in windowboxes to add splashes of colour.

RIGHT Make a strong display of rich bright reds with *Geum* 'Mrs J. Bradshaw', *Lychnis chalcedonica* and *Rosa* 'Fragrant Cloud'.

# fiery reds

**If you're going to use red,** you've got to have one or two plants in pillar box or fire engine red that take the colour up to its limit. Group a few dark reds together using plants like *Cosmos atrosanguineus*, whose flowers smell on hot sunny days of chocolate, mourning widow (*Geranium phaeum*), and *Knautia macedonica*, which produces a fantastic mass of pincushion reds all summer, then inject vermillion in the middle. If you want to keep the scarlet theme running on into late autumn, make sure that you have a Japanese maple (*Acer palmatum*) like 'Komon nishiki' or 'Matsukaze', whose leaves flare into the most extraordinary scarlet before the winter comes crashing in.

# pink

Soft pink is an excellent colour for calming down the garden, but sharp or strong pink is on the verge of being bright red. Soft pinks rarely work well in large groups because they can be extremely timid, but they are a great way of building up to something much more dramatic. Note that some pinks can change colour markedly in different lights. Soft pinks whiten out in full sun, while they gain extra richness at twilight. Also, some pink plants offer excellent scent.

At the top of the list are *Viburnum* x *bodnantense*, which flowers over winter, the daphnes, especially *Daphne bholua* 'Jacqueline Postill' in late winter, sweet peas (*Lathyrus*), and lilies and roses at the height of summer. Using scented plants is an extra way of making sure that the flowers are really noticed.

*Pelargonium* 'Rollisson's Unique'

# dark pink

Rich, dark pinks come in all shapes and sizes, from low, flat ground cover giving a wide mat between large shrubs and a vista right across the garden, to taller, obtrusive shrubs that can foreshorten a view with rich colour. There's also a chance to add tall spires such as foxgloves (*Digitalis*), and some superb plants such as bougainvillea which provide a fantastic array of hues.

ABOVE *Camellia* 'Elizabeth Hawkins' is a smart bright pink that immediately perks up the garden.

ABOVE The reddish-pink flowers of *Helianthemum* 'Sudbury Red' offer a splash of colour in a rockery.

ABOVE *Clematis* 'Allanah' is well worth getting for its fantastic bright reddish-pink flowers and black anthers.

ABOVE Honesty (*Lunaria annua*) gives near purple flowers from late spring on, growing about 90cm (3ft) high.

ABOVE Foxgloves (*Digitalis*) rarely look out of place in the border, where they shoot up in summer.

ABOVE Tall, bright perennial lupins (*Lupinus*), such as this one in lipstick pink, make very good 'eye-catchers'.

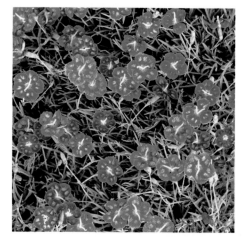

ABOVE Pinks (*Dianthus*) make super cut flowers, and give terrific displays in sunny gardens with good drainage.

ABOVE *Rhododendron* 'Hydon Dawn' is a big-value, small, compact shrub, with masses of pink flowers.

ABOVE *Rosa* 'Hansa' has large, highly scented blooms tinged reddish-violet, followed by impressive hips.

ABOVE If you've got room in your conservatory, a free-flowering bougainvillea is a must.

ABOVE Alliums offer some of the best excitement in the early summer garden; many are shaped like drumsticks.

ABOVE Cantabrian heath (*Daboecia cantabrica* 'Atropurpurea') provides excellent ground cover and colour.

ABOVE Campion (*Silene armeria* 'Electra') is a free-flowering deep pink that gives a late summer show.

ABOVE 'Jer'Rey' is an excellent two-tone pelargonium that creates a strong display on its own.

ABOVE *Pelargonium* 'Rollisson's Unique' can grow 45cm (18in) high, and looks best highlighted in a pot.

ABOVE *Lampranthus* need dry conditions and are perfect for rock crevices or well-drained rockeries.

# hot pink

**The sharper kinds of pink** are nearly on a par with purple, and can be used in big bold shows by growing large shrubs and climbers. In fact using this rich, zingy colour gives you a chance to include some high performance plants from spring to autumn.

Start off the show with a rhododendron like the award-winning 'Rose Bud', which has rose-pink flowers in spring, and follow it with a range of summer roses. 'Zéphirine Drouhin', 3.6m (12ft) high, has the three virtues of being highly scented, thornless and happy on north walls, while the slightly shorter 'Pink Perpétué' is good climbing up a pillar. The geraniums give a huge range of pinks in the border, with *Geranium* x *riversleaianum* 'Russell Pritchard' being one of the strongest. In the autumn, aim for swathes of *Colchicum speciosum* under deciduous trees, which stand out all the more because the flowers open before the leaves begin to appear. Make sure that all the strong pinks get a chance to stand out by keeping them well away from any sharper colours.

TOP **Pinks (*Dianthus*) work well with shamrock (*Oxalis*) in this old copper bucket.**

ABOVE **High impact displays of gladioli need a sheltered sunny spot with good drainage.**

FAR RIGHT **Azaleas love acid soil and make a startling show in late spring.**

deep beds filled with **glossy** pink **perenials**

# Mexican painted pots

## You Will Need

**Fluted-top garden pot**

**Masking tape**

**White undercoat paint**

**Small decorating brush**

**Gouache poster colours**

**2 artists' brushes, one
very fine**

**Polyurethane varnish**

**Red or dark pink
pelargoniums**

Garden containers can sometimes be dull and it is fun to brighten them up to create a splash of colour on your patio or windowbox. The inspiration here was Mexican motifs but you can be inventive and try different designs. Complete the effect by planting up the pots with vibrant pelargoniums in brilliant reds and pinks.

**1** Mark the stripes on the pot using masking tape. Vary the widths of the tape to get variation in the finished design. Bear in mind that the areas covered will remain natural terracotta.

**3** Paint the coloured stripes, changing colour after each band of masking tape. Allow to dry completely. Peel off the masking tape to reveal coloured stripes alternating with the terracotta.

**2** Completely paint the main body of the pot with undercoat, painting over the masking tape as well. Allow to dry according to the manufacturer's instructions.

**4** Using the fine artist's brush and the undercoat, paint simple motifs over the stripes. When completely dry, coat the painted area with varnish.

# pale pink

Pale pinks and peachy colours are on offer at all heights, from down by your ankle to climbers high in the trees. Being soft and quiet they are unobtrusive and yet demand a closer look, so it is well worth giving them extra space where you can appreciate their form and texture. The fuchsias in particular always attract plenty of praise.

ABOVE There are dozens of exquisite pink camellias; many are quite tender and need a conservatory.

ABOVE Tulips come in all shapes and sizes; don't overlook little beauties like this.

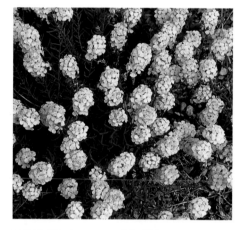

ABOVE Stone cress (*Aethionema grandiflorum*) is a 25cm (10in) high perennial for a late spring show.

ABOVE *Camellia* 'Lady Loch' is a genuine beauty making a rounded shape covered with pale pink flowers.

ABOVE If you like the large-flowering *Clematis* 'Nelly Moser', try 'Bees Jubilee' because it's even brighter.

ABOVE *Rhododendron* 'Pink Pearl' makes a big, open shape, and is a real eye catcher in the spring.

ABOVE Autumn crocuses (*Colchicum*) provide a cheerful splash of colour when many plants are past flowering.

ABOVE *Rosa* 'Albertine' is a prolific rambler with salmon-pink flowers that readily grows 6m (20ft) high.

ABOVE Tender rose bay (*Nerium oleander*) flowers in summer. It is a good choice for conservatories.

ABOVE Like most pot plants, begonias can be stood outside over summer to inject colour into any gaps.

ABOVE Not all poppies (*Papaver*) have gutsy, blood-red flowers; many are gentle pastels.

ABOVE Fuchsias such as 'Silver Dawn' add a different scale to the garden with their soft-coloured flowers.

ABOVE Stonecrop (*Sedum*) is a big-value, fail-safe summer and autumn plant, providing a big show of flowers.

ABOVE *Verbena* 'Peaches and Cream' is an increasingly popular annual with spreading branching growth.

ABOVE *Rosa* 'Breath of Life' is a scented mini-climber that will not grow much higher than 2.4m (8ft).

ABOVE *Fuchsia* 'Monterey' has a strong vivid colour, and flowers that resemble hovering insects.

# gentle pink

**Soft, gentle pink is a highly underrated colour.** If your garden suffers from any harsh outrageous features, trail soft pink climbers all over them, or group pots of pink fuchsias around them, to achieve an immediate transformation. It is also well worth growing one or two really exquisite special pinks in pots for standing on a terrace or eating area, where they will catch the eye and act as a kind of instant, elaborate flower arrangement. The key point with shapely pinks though, is not to lose them against a massed background in the border. Give them room to show off. And place the autumn-flowering pinks where the sun's more orange rays will catch them, giving them extra warmth and glow.

fresh **inspiring**
shades of **spring** pink

RIGHT 'Cotton Candy' is one of the very best fuchsias. It is free-flowering, of medium height, and has a sprightly, upright shape. Regular 'pinching out' encourages even more flowers.

FAR RIGHT TOP *Rosa* 'Ispahan' is a choice, old-fashioned Damask rose that has scented pink flowers. It is one of the best of its kind because it has a long flowering period.

FAR RIGHT BOTTOM Hebes can make big shrubs, but there are many small ones that are ideal for pots. Painting the container helps bring out the colour of the flowers.

# blue

Woodland bluebells (*Hyacinthoides*) are a terrific sight, not because they're growing in any way 'naturally' and free, but because of three key factors. First, the colour stands out that much more in light shade, second, it is highlighted by a light green grassy background and third, the bluebells spread in large numbers and take the eye further and further away. While it's hard to repeat the last point in the garden, you can aim to give the blues some slight degree of shade to make them stand out even more brightly and vividly. When arranging blues, note that other plants can be used to nudge them into the foreground, just as blues can be used to highlight whites. One of the very best royal blues for the garden is *Anchusa azurea* 'Loddon Royalist'. It has got to be top of your list.

*Iris* 'Dusky Challenger'

# purple-blue

There is no excuse for not having plenty of rich dark blues and purples in the garden. You can use it as a special feature, letting the annual morning glory (*Ipomoea*) scramble up a wigwam of canes, spreading as a carpet on the ground with Dalmatian bellflower (*Campanula portenschlagiana*), or in bushes of scented French lavender (*Lavandula stoechas*).

ABOVE **One of the most gorgeous ipomoeas, Morning glory (*Ipomoea indica*) is easily grown from seed.**

ABOVE *Lavandula pinnata*, originally from the Canary Islands, is a late summer-flowering shrub.

ABOVE *Vinca minor* 'Aureovariegata' gives first-rate ground cover and masses of blue flowers all summer.

ABOVE French lavender (*Lavandula stoechas*) is small and bushy with masses of dark purple flowers.

ABOVE **There is a great range of blue geraniums that thrive just about anywhere, giving colour all summer.**

ABOVE **The violet flowers of the annual *Nicandra physalodes* are followed by masses of berries.**

ABOVE **The blue bellflower *Campanula carpatica* produces open, disc-like flowers all summer.**

ABOVE *Anemone blanda* is one of the best slightly purple perennials for livening up the spring garden.

ABOVE *Triteleia laxa* gives a good show in early summer, but it needs a sunny position and hates frost.

ABOVE Crocuses can provide colour for nine months of the year; *Crocus nudiflorus* is the one for autumn.

ABOVE Dalmatian bellflower (*Campanula portenschlagiana*) is a robust evergreen about ankle high.

ABOVE The clear, soft blue flowers of *Iris pallida* subsp. *pallida* emerge from beautiful silvery bracts in spring.

ABOVE Jerusalem sage (*Pulmonaria saccharata*) gives two-tone spring colour and has attractive leaves.

ABOVE The mourning widow (*Geranium phaeum*) has such deep purple flowers that they look black.

ABOVE The flowers of *Rhododendron* 'Penheale Blue' are slightly violet-blue when they open in early spring.

ABOVE The blue flag iris (*Iris versicolor*) makes tall flowering clumps round the edge of a pond.

# indigo blue

**You need to have several great blues** in the garden in each season to set off the rest of the planting. The good news is that there are plenty of first-rate plants. In spring the California lilac (*Ceanothus* 'Blue Mound') erupts in a great 1.5m (5ft) high mound, though if you fancy a bigger show *Ceanothus arboreus* 'Trewithen Blue' can cover 6 x 8m (20 x 25ft). In summer you can let clematis romp up pillars and posts, and use the likes of buddleja to provide an aerial mass of blue flowers that attract thousands of butterflies. *Salvia uliginosa* starts performing in late summer with long thin open stems topped by bright pale blue flowers. Contrast any darker blues with whites and yellows to highlight their rich tones.

ABOVE When you think the garden is full up, start adding vertical structures and you can send up a huge range of colourful climbers, such as this flamboyant clematis.

LEFT Grape hyacinths (*Muscari latifolium*) offer a wonderful, rich deep blue and look good in clumps in borders or patio pots.

RIGHT These vivid convolvulus are beautifully set off by the blue rim of the pot.

# springtime blues

**You Will Need**

1 medium to large blue pot
selection of old crocks or
large stones
soil-based compost
(soil mix)
10 pretty pink, midseason
tulips such as Tulipa 'Ester'
4 Viola x wittrockiana
(pansy) such as two-toned
'Marina', 'Violet with
Blotch', 'Light Blue' or
'True Blue'

Blues, mauves and pinks are pretty, fresh colours that are easy on the eye in spring. This sky-blue container sets off the soft mauves and pinks of the pansies and tulips beautifully; similar containers can be found at most garden centres. The same effect can also be created when planting up a windowbox.

**1** Cover the base of the pot with a 5cm (2in) layer of drainage material, such as old crocks. Half-fill the pot with a soil-based compost (soil mix) containing lots of grit, vital for drainage.

**3** Plant the ten tulip bulbs in two circles, spacing them out evenly and making sure they are not touching each other or the sides of the pot, so they have plenty of room for growth.

**2** If you prefer, as an alternative, use a peat-based compost (soil mix) with a layer of grit mixed thoroughly in the bottom half, again to ensure good drainage in winter.

**4** Bring the compost level to within 2.5cm (1in) of the top of the pot. Plant the four winter-flowering pansies. The result is a glorious spring display of soft pinks and blues.

# mauve-blue

The blues and purples might be the plants that catch the eye, and they're clearly rich, powerful colours, but too many together can end up being slightly gloomy. Include some paler, lighter mauves because these are extremely good for brightening things up. They do need to be grouped with great care, however, as their effect can be lost against a pale or whitish background. Place plants with beautiful, interesting shapes, such as the North American *Camassia cusickii*, in front of darker backgrounds that will really show them up.

ABOVE *Clematis* 'Mrs Cholmondeley' flourishes in early summer with a mass of light mauve flowers.

ABOVE Bindweed (*Convolvulus sabatius*) needs a fast-draining sunny position to flower all summer.

ABOVE The pale blue, scented chimney bellflower (*Campanula pyramidalis*) loves dry, sunny parts of the garden.

ABOVE *Aster* x *frikartii* 'Monch' makes a superb clump of light blue flowers in late summer and early autumn.

ABOVE The Spanish/North African *Geranium malviflorum* with wide, red-veined, pale blue flowers.

ABOVE This alpine *Campanula* will spread to create a blue carpet of tiny, blue, star-like flowers.

ABOVE *Corydalis flexuosa* thrives in shady, rich, well-drained soil, and can also be planted in rockeries.

ABOVE For ground cover with a difference, try *Pratia pedunculata* which thrives even in hot, dry weather.

ABOVE Sweet William (*Phlox divaricata*) flowers in early summer in a wide range of colours, including pale blue.

ABOVE The clump-forming *Scilla peruviana* has a lovely spread of star-shaped flowers in early summer.

ABOVE Prostrate speedwell (*Veronica prostrata*) quickly spreads, making a low carpet of early summer flowers.

ABOVE Baby blue eyes (*Nemophila menziesii*) is an American annual with bright blue flowers.

ABOVE One of the key plants in any blue border is the highly popular *Sisyrinchium* 'California Skies'.

ABOVE The Spanish bluebell (*Hyacinthoides hispanica*) makes a terrific show in a damp, shady spot.

ABOVE *Camassia cusickii* peps things up in late spring with pale blue flowers on top of 75cm (30in) spikes.

# calming mauve

**Mauve is cool and chic.** It is the best colour for giving parts of the garden a clear-cut, elegant theme. Formal, stylized lawns with statues and urns, window boxes against whitewashed houses, and minimalist gardens where shape counts much more than the planting, are all prime contenders for the wide range of mauves available. Mix them with soft pastels such as pinks, greys and cream for the best results.

You can also use mauve in blocks at repeat intervals to act as dividers along a border with much brasher colours, and to highlight and be highlighted by neighbouring stronger tones in a mixed scheme.

## **restful** and soothing **waves** of mauve

RIGHT The architectural style of the garden is emphasized by the use of an urn on a pedestal, and a knot garden with interweaving patterns. The surrounding colour scheme is unashamedly gorgeous, using a mass of lavender (*Lavandula*).

FAR RIGHT TOP  Frame statues that could otherwise be lost to view with thin, elegant spires of colour, using soft pastels that will enhance and not compete with the figure.

FAR RIGHT BOTTOM Flowering window boxes are an excellent way of softening a white exterior. You only need a few attractive plants that flower through the summer to achieve this simple, stylish effect.

# white

White might not seem like a colour, but it is; it is actually made up of all the other colours combined, and that's why white goes with anything. You could even try to make a white garden, but if you aim for exclusively white you'll find the glare of midsummer can make it unremittingly forceful and hard. It would be far better to make the garden largely white, injecting plenty of other colours to add rich contrasts during the day. The white stands out in a near magical way at dusk, though, as if the flowers were tiny light bulbs. This effect is most thrilling when a white climbing rose, dangling high out a tree, is lit by a full moon. And because white is such a dominant, forceful colour it is worth checking that the plants are shapely and worth a much closer look. White is one colour that really does capture the eye.

*Allium sativum*

# white

Whites don't have to be in solid blocks to make a great feature, extraordinarily beautiful though flowers such as lilies and roses are. Whites can create tall, thin verticals, with foxgloves (*Digitalis*), and in the case of *Crambe cordifolia* a fantastic aerial speckling of hundreds of tiny white flowers during the first half of summer.

ABOVE *Rosa* 'Climbing Iceberg' easily grows 3m (10ft) high, and produces lashings of flowers all summer.

ABOVE *Rosa* 'Pascali' is white with a dash of cream, and provides a fine supply of highly attractive flowers.

ABOVE This 1.5m (5ft) high *Dahlia* 'Porcelain' with a hint of lilac is best grown at the back of the border.

ABOVE The rock garden is the best place for this low-growing early summer *Saxifraga paniculata*.

ABOVE Common white foxgloves (*Digitalis purpurea*) really stand out among brighter colours.

ABOVE *Galtonia candicans* is a big-value, tall South African perennial that flowers at the end of summer.

ABOVE Patches of *Allium nigrum*, often with a lilac tinge, make a terrific sight in the early summer border.

ABOVE Cantabrian heath (*Daboecia cantabrica* 'Snowdrift') continues to flower all summer long.

ABOVE Foxtail lilies (*Eremurus*) spice things up with late spring spires that can reach 3m (10ft) high.

ABOVE *Arabis caucasica* 'Flore Pleno' is a rare plant that has pure white, scented flowers.

ABOVE *Crambe cordifolia* has criss-cross stems, creating an aerial balloon, with scores of tiny flowers.

ABOVE *Rhododendron decorum* stages a spectacular late spring to early summer show with scented flowers.

ABOVE *Achillea ageratifolia* produces a mass of flowers that make a fine low link at the front of the border.

ABOVE *Camellia* 'Cornish Snow' grows into a big shrub, packed with flowers that are tinged pink on opening.

ABOVE *Osteospermum caulescens* keeps low and spreads wide, creating a mat of daisy-like flowers.

ABOVE There are many lilies in white and cream, the more intriguing ones with a speckling along the petals.

# clean whites

**If you think spring has to mean yellow**, that is daffodils, daffodils and more daffodils, you're mistaken. There are plenty of quite beautiful whites to start off the new year. Stylish tulips take some beating, like 'Spring Green' and the extremely popular 'White Triumphator', which has a beautiful slender flower that stands about 60cm (2ft) high. White tulips are best highlighted by dwarf box (*Buxus*) hedging or a dark green background such as yew (*Taxus*). Other star white spring plants include anemones, camellias, *Clematis armandii*, magnolias and ornamental cherry (*Prunus*).

LEFT *Rhododendron* 'Loder's White' offers a burst of fresh colour in spring.

ABOVE Lily-of-the-valley (*Convallaria majalis*) makes exquisitely scented ground cover.

RIGHT The taller tulips always look better when they are underplanted with a complementary colour, like these white daisies.

# summery whites

**Gardens need fresh, summery whites** to lift
and brighten displays, and also to provide an instant,
highly effective contrast that will emphasize magentas,
dark reds and  yellows. It gives an all-round spark. You
can either stick to individual plants that will hold their
own, keep their shape and remain completely distinct,
or opt for twisters, scramblers and climbers that don't
have to grow vertically, but can happily spiral their way
horizontally through and over adjacent plants. Use
medium-sized shrubs to give clematis and roses a leg-up,
and to provide a horticultural shelf for them to charge over.

# **romantic** shades
## of summery **white**

FAR LEFT While the large-flowering roses catch the eye, smaller, delicate, more elegant ones are at times just what you need to create the perfect display.

LEFT Plant *Solanum jasminoides* 'Album' next to an evergreen, such as a holly, and let it scramble its way up, making a great showy mass of white flowers all summer.

BELOW The white flowers of these tobacco plants (*Nicotiana*) and heliotrope (*Heliotropium*) leap out with even more gusto than normal because of the contrasting terracotta colouring and the abundant rich green leaves.

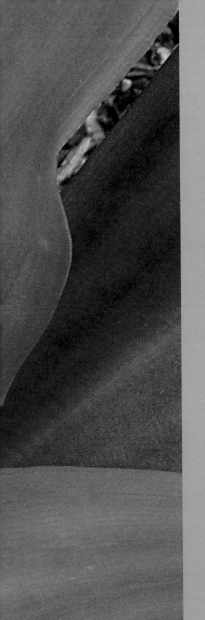

# green

You might not see green as a colour for high summer when the rest of the garden is in top gear, but in spring, after months of mud and splatter, the massive eruption of fresh green foliage makes it the most invigorating sight of the year. This is when green is the star colour, but thereafter it becomes a backdrop, setting off everything else. Not that it has to be. If you choose striking, shapely plants, they'll get as much attention as anything else will. *Gunnera manicata* has strong vertical stems and rough crinkly leaves, like flattened satellite dishes just above your head. You'll also need plenty of evergreens, such as Mexican orange blossom (*Choisya ternata*), to keep the garden alive out of season; the shinier the leaves the better to make the most of the winter sun.

*Eucomis bicolor*

# dark green

Dark green is an exceptional background colour to make white or pale flowers really stand out, and for that you need at least one preferably evergreen shrub or bamboo. The contrast can be just as effective using smart variegated foliage where the leaves have strong white or cream markings. And where you get rich green leaves topped by white, the effect is even better.

ABOVE **Grow sages in herb gardens and in any good border, using them to link all kinds of colour schemes.**

ABOVE **Yew (*Taxus baccata*), makes great topiary and an excellent dark background for white flowers.**

ABOVE **'June' is a terrific new hosta that mixes rich blue-green colouring with yellow around the middle.**

ABOVE **Greek oregano (above) and marjoram are closely related, but the former has the stronger scent.**

ABOVE *Hedera helix* **'Congesta' is a non-climbing ivy that makes a small, neat bush about 45cm (18in) high.**

ABOVE **Common tansy (*Tanacetum vulgare*) has shapely, elegant leaves and bright yellow summer flowers.**

ABOVE *Pseudosasa japonica* **is a first-rate bamboo that makes a tall thicket with shiny dark green leaves.**

ABOVE The Japanese painted fern (*Athyrium niponicum* var. 'Pictum') has wonderful bluish-green leaves.

ABOVE *Hosta ventricosa* 'Variegata' has spinach green leaves with a cream margin.

ABOVE *Sasa palmata* is a Japanese bamboo that normally reaches 6m (20ft), but twice that in dense shade.

ABOVE *Hosta undulata* becomes known as *H. u.* var. *univittata* when the central white stripe appears.

ABOVE The bamboo *Pleioblastus simonii* 'Variegatus' has striped, pointy leaves up to 20cm (8in) long.

ABOVE *Shibataea kumasasa* is a slender-stemmed bamboo, which forms mounds of dark green foliage.

ABOVE Aleutian maidenhair fern (*Adiantum aleuticum*) perks up any semi-shady area with its fine fronds.

ABOVE *Sasa veitchii* is a moderate 1.5m (5ft) high bamboo that romps through woods in the wild.

ABOVE *Levisticum officinale* is a shapely, strong-growing perennial with yellowish flowers in midsummer.

# forest green

**Rich, lively, jungle greens** are a brilliant way of creating an instant atmosphere. You can either go the whole way – using layers and layers of plants, building them up from the ground, ending up with climbers and trees – or you can be much more subtle. A few ferns in any shady spot gives immediate extra interest, while topiary balls, pyramids, spirals and cones add year-round style and impact. You can use the latter as extra, moveable features, or to enliven any flight of steps. You could even create one long, flowing shape, like a sinuous, baroque kind of octopus, by growing it in several sections, each plant in its own container.

deep beds filled with **luscious, verdant** foliage

ABOVE LEFT A good mix of ferns and hostas (in the bottom right-hand corner). Hostas are invariably grown for their marvellous leaves, many of which have excellent white markings.

LEFT Topiary box (*Buxus*) plants are readily available in most garden centres. Alternatively, you can clip the plants into shape yourself.

RIGHT Any garden can be given a Victorian makeover with a few simple ingredients such as a statue and ferns.

# green mosaic table

## You Will Need

Tracing paper and pencil
Marine plywood or exterior
grade plywood, 13mm
(1/2 in) thick
PVA (white) glue
Paintbrush
Glass mosaic tiles in off-
white, light verdigris, dark
verdigris, moss, gold-veined
verdigris, gold-veined green
Tile nippers
Goggles
Flexible knife
Cement-based, water-
resistant tile adhesive
Cement-based, water-
resistant grout
Small bucket
Grout spreader
Sponge and soft cloth
Rubber gloves

The soft greens and golds used in the simple flower design of this mosaic table make for a striking piece of furniture, which looks great with lush foliage. It can be used outdoors in good weather, but you will need to bring it inside during very rainy periods and for the winter because it is not completely weatherproof.

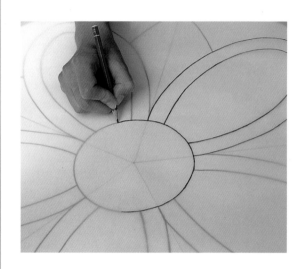

1 Mark out the design for the tabletop, then transfer it to a large sheet of tracing paper. Turn the tracing paper upside down onto the plywood and rub the pattern through to the wood.

3 Mix up the tile adhesive and spread a thin layer over one area at a time. Select the tiles you want and press them into the tile adhesive, leaving a tiny gap between each piece.

2 Seal the marked out plywood with the PVA (white) glue, then cut the tiles into small pieces using tile nippers. Make a pile of each colour and save some to chip into different sizes later on.

4 Scatter the gold-veined tiles among the plain ones to create a subtle sheen. To achieve a neat finish around corners, clip the tiles into wedge shapes with the tile nippers.

# an **elegant** table
# perfect for a **lush** garden

5 Continue to fill in the whole design, using the tile nippers to trim the tiles so they fit snugly into the pattern. Once it is complete, leave the tabletop to dry for at least a day.

6 Mix the grout and push it into all the cracks. Wipe over with a damp sponge and polish with a dry cloth. Once dry, turn the tabletop over and spread the base with adhesive to seal it.

# pale green

Every good garden should have a selection of evergreens with differently shaped leaves to link up the summer plants, and to keep the garden alive in winter. It is essential that you make sure that one green tone does not dominate though. Adding lime greens, pale greens, olive greens, cabbage greens etc, will give a much wider, more relaxed range of hues.

ABOVE *Hosta* 'Birchwood Parky's Gold' has yellow-green leaves that give a lift to shady parts of the garden.

ABOVE Ivy (*Hedera helix* 'Golden Ingot') creates a fresh summery look, and is good on long, low walls.

ABOVE The lovely lime-coloured, white-edged leaves of *Hosta* 'Shade Fanfare' turn even paler with age.

ABOVE There are hundreds of different ivies (*Hedera*) in all shades, and the lighter ones make a good backdrop.

ABOVE Architectural plants such as grasses come in a wide range of pale green shades.

ABOVE Lime-green euphorbia is invaluable, providing highlights and contrast in a strong colour scheme.

ABOVE Grasses are back in fashion, such as this *Carex hachijoensis*, which makes a small, lush mound.

ABOVE *Arundo donax* is not in fact a bamboo, but a perennial grass that can grow to 5m (15ft) high.

ABOVE *Pelargonium* 'Mr Henry Cox' is one of the best of its kind if you want patterned leaves with green.

ABOVE Japanese rush (*Acorus gramineus*), an aquatic perennial, adds glossy green colour to ponds.

ABOVE *Gunnera manicata* is ideal if you have a big, damp, boggy space where it can open its massive leaves.

ABOVE *Helichrysum petiolare* is a low, spreading evergreen with white flowers at the end of summer.

ABOVE Italian buckthorn (*Rhamnus alaternus* 'Argenteovariegata') has good foliage, flowers and red fruit.

ABOVE *Pennisetum orientale* is a small grass with beautiful spikelets tinged with a faint purple colour.

ABOVE Silvery-leaved lamb's ears (*Stachys byzantina*) mixes well with this blue-flowering *Nepeta*.

ABOVE The eye-catching *Eryngium giganteum* has spiky green foliage and pale, silvery blue flowers.

# mellow green

**When you can't decide** what colour goes right next to a dark or blue-leaved plant, take the colour scheme down a notch by adding a superb pale green. From the blue-tinged kind to ones with a yellowish hue, they add a sense of quiet and space, a pause in the mood of the garden. Conifers, from tiny, hard compact mounds to tall evergreen, vertical chopsticks, are very useful and come in every shade of green, some even verging on black. They also add a sharp sculptural feel. Euphorbias are even livelier, many having smart shapes and pale green involucres like tiny saucers at the tops of the stems. Soft, mellow green is incredibly versatile. Grow it, link it, try it.

FAR LEFT  A sensational display of grasses offer soothing colours as well as architectural interest.

ABOVE LEFT A grouping of conifers in the fore-ground, with variegated hostas behind.

ABOVE RIGHT A shady, quiet corner is livened up by an attractive fern.

# colour
# combinations

The key to a look like this (left) is to make sure you grow plants in lively, contrasting blocks of colour. Tulips give the most astonishing spring displays, and they can be as jazzy or as cool as you like. You can underplant the whole scheme with forget-me-nots (*Myosotis sylvatica*), which provide a blue backing. If you want to see how you can upgrade the scheme, ignore all talk about taste and fashion and see what artists like Jackson Pollock and van Gogh did with a paintbrush.

Be brave, mix colours and make sure you grab the eye. Whether you choose the classic combinations of blue and white, or red and yellow, or more exciting mixtures of purple and orange, or lime green and turquoise, the possibilities are endless.

# classics

**Some colour combinations are always good**, no matter where they are grown. Yellow and blue, red and white, blue and pink, paired up these always look sensational. The trick is to spot which colours and which plants work well in major gardens, and then to copy the idea in your own garden. Huge houses with 55 acres might be able to provide a better backdrop and more elaborate scale, but all gardening means reinventing, rescaling and adapting ideas to suit your needs. And if the combinations do work, put them right at the front where they will "carry" any neighbouring plants and give them a special lift.

## snappy, **primary** shades create **stunning** borders

ABOVE Two rows, two colours, and the result is totally stylish.

LEFT A wide mix of traditional blooms gives an easy flow.

RIGHT A smart group of 'Striped Belladonna' tulips.

# pastels

**Every garden needs quiet,** exquisite moments
using soft pinks, white and mauve. Such schemes work
infinitely better if they are given plenty of space where
they can create their own special mood; they should
not be crammed into a spare hidden corner. The scheme
will be even more sumptuous if you can include plenty
of plants that have rich scents; mock orange blossom
(*Philadelphus*) and old shrub roses such as *Rosa* 'Charles
de Mills' are essential.

# **soothing** and **calming** blues and creams

FAR LEFT An enterprising mix of love-in-a-mist (*Nigella damascena*), with a sensational cream-coloured climbing rose.

LEFT Flatter an interesting statue with pastel roses, clematis and foxgloves (*Digitalis*).

BELOW A two-tone classic summer combination using a swirl of pale cream roses set off by blue phlox.

ABOVE **Flash-red Dahlia 'Bishop of Llandaff'**
**backed by blue asters.**

LEFT **Purple alliums and orange *Eremurus***
**provide complementary shapes.**

RIGHT **A stunning display of Himalayan blue**
**poppies (*Meconopsis*), lime-green euphorbia**
**and orange 'Warm Welcome' climbing rose.**

# contemporary

**The colourful garden of the 21st century needs shape and style,** and
a "look-at-me-now" air. Use bright, strong colours in challenging, unexpected ways. Architectural
plants with zany stems and blobs of colour on top need their own space where their look can
unfold. Also, go for strong contrasts using just two colours; don't let visitors rest in a stupefying
soft soup of pastels designed to send them to sleep. Keep their eyes alert, bring primary colours
up close and then use them far away. Best of all, work with and then break their assumptions.
Use colour in the garden as if it were brand new.

# seasonal gardening tips

## SPRING

### What to Plant

- Container-grown trees and shrubs
- Gladioli and summer bulbs
- Hanging baskets
- Hedges
- Herbaceous plants and stake them
- Sweet peas sown last autumn
- Finish planting bare-rooted trees and shrubs
- Divide dahlia tubers that have started sprouting
- Divide and replant congested vigorous perennials

**Furniture and other accessories can be used to inject colour into a garden as well as plants**

### What to Prune

- Dogwoods (*Cornus*), thinning them out
- *Eucalyptus gunnii*, for a supply of new coloured stems
- Evergreen shrubs that need clipping
- Overgrown deciduous hedges
- Roses, if they have not already been done
- Shrubs that flower on new growth (eg buddlejas)
- Winter-flowering heathers
- Pinch out the tips of fuchsias to make them bush out, or train them as standards

### What to Sow

- Hardy annuals
- Harden off tender bedding plants

### What to Feed

- Add slow-release fertilizer to the compost of container plants
- Beds and borders while wet after heavy rain

### Lawns and Ponds

- Make a new lawn from seed or turf, and repair worn patches
- Mow established lawns regularly from now on starting with a high cut
- Plant and stock new ponds with oxygenators

### Extras

- Beware of late frosts and protect tender growth
- Spring clean and ventilate the greenhouse
- Deadhead the flowers of bulbs, and let the foliage die down naturally

- Tidy up the rock garden, and apply fresh stone chippings where necessary

## SUMMER

### In the Flower Garden

- Finish hardening off and planting out tender bedding plants
- Dead-head plants in borders and containers regularly
- Plant dahlias and later give a tomato feed, and water regularly
- Hoe beds and borders to eliminate weeds
- Lift and store tulip bulbs
- Mow lawns planted with spring bulbs
- Plant autumn-flowering bulbs (eg colchicums)
- Plant out summer bedding
- Buy new plants
- Tie in new shoots on climbers
- Thin hardy annuals
- Watch for signs of mildew and aphids on roses, and spray promptly if found
- Apply a rose fertilizer once the main flush of flowering is over

### What to Propagate

- Layer border carnations
- Start sowing hardy annuals to overwinter
- Take semi-ripe cuttings of fuchsias and pelargoniums, etc; early and midsummer are the best times to propagate

### What to Sow

- Biennials such as wallflowers and forget-me-nots
- Fast-growing annuals such as sunflowers

This rich mixture of yellows, reds and blues has created a stunning summer patio border

### What to Prune

- Clip beech, holly, hornbeam and yew hedges, etc
- Cut back and feed delphiniums and lupins after flowering to get a second batch of flowers
- Pinch out the growing tip from early-flowering chrysanthemums
- Broom, lilac, philadelphus, spiraea, wisteria, etc., and exhausted rambler roses after flowering

### Lawns and Ponds

- Remove excessive growth of algae in ponds, leaving some for young frogs to hide in

• Make sure frogs and newts can easily get out of ponds, and add nearby hiding places

• Mow the lawn, except in very dry weather, and never scalp it

• Top up water levels in ponds. Only add fish if you haven't got frogs, or they'll eat all the young

### Extras

• Go on nightly patrols armed with a torch and bucket, and remove/destroy slugs and snails

• Order bulb catalogues and spring-flowering bulbs for autumn delivery

• Ventilate greenhouses every day, more so when hot, and water regularly

*Tulipa kolpakowskiana*

# AUTUMN

### In the Flower Garden

• Collect ripe seed, and store in airtight containers

• Cut down and lift dahlias blackened by frost; store for next year

• Cut down the dead tops of herbaceous perennials

• Lift and store gladioli and other tender bulbs, corms and tubers

• Lift and take in chrysanthemums not hardy enough to overwinter outside

### What to Plant

• Bare-rooted shrubs and winter trees (including roses) from now to late winter

• Lilies, and spring-flowering bulbs such as tulips

• Winter window boxes

• Climbers

### What to Sow

• Garlic cloves

• Spring-flowering biennials

• Sweet peas for planting out next spring

### Lawns and Ponds

• Clear fallen leaves and debris out of ponds

• Rake lawns

• Sow new lawns

### Extras

• Clean out and insulate greenhouses

• Clear summer bedding and prepare for spring bedding plants

• Collect and compost fallen leaves

## WINTER

### What to Plant

- Continue planting bare-rooted shrubs and trees
- Divide clumps of snowdrops while still in leaf

### What to Prune

- Wisteria
- Roses in late winter
- Cut back grasses

### Extras

- Build compost heaps
- Check bulbs that have been stored

**Rich pink flowers in contrasting tones, such as these azaleas, add a brilliant splash of colour to any border**

- Protect slightly tender plants such as some penstemons in cold spells
- Check spring catalogues have been ordered
- Make sure the greenhouse is ventilated even during cold weather when paraffin heaters are used
- Ensure there is enough winter colour in the garden, and plan for next year if there isn't
- If you want to, change the garden's design, or embellish with extra features such as ornamental paths, ponds (but do not line until next spring), pergolas, etc.

# planting guide

This is a checklist of plants that, together with those in the portrait galleries, provide key blocks or flashes of colour. Plants that require ericaceous or acid soil are indicated by an asterisk.

## SPRING

### Yellow

*Adonis amurensis*

Primrose (*Primula*)

*Crocus*

Crown imperial (*Fritillaria*)

Daffodil (*Narcissus*)

*Forsythia*

Peony (*Paeonia*)

***Rosa* 'Just Joey'**

*Rhododendron* (including azalea)*

Skunk cabbage (*Lysichiton americanus*)

Tulip (*Tulipa*)

Wallflower (*Erysimum*)

### Orange

Crown imperial (*Fritillaria*)

Daffodil (*Narcissus*)

*Physalis*

*Rhododendron* (including azalea)*

Tulip (*Tulipa*)

Wallflower (*Erysimum*)

### Red

*Anemone*

*Bellis perennis*

*Chaenomeles*

Lenten rose (*Helleborus orientalis*)

Peony (*Paeonia*)

Tulip (*Tulipa*)

### Pink

*Bergenia* x *schmidtii*

*Camellia sasanqua*

Cowslip, primrose (*Primula*)

Crab apple (*Malus*)

*Cyclamen coum*

*Daphne*

Hellebore (*Helleborus orientalis*)

*Nectaroscordum siculum* subsp. *bulgaricum*

Ornamental cherry – blossom (*Prunus*)

Peony (*Paeonia*)

*Pulmonaria*

*Rhododendron* (including azalea)*

Tulip (*Tulipa*)

### Blue

*Anemone blanda*

Bluebell (*Hyacinthoides*)

California lilac (*Ceanothus*)

*Clematis alpina* 'Frances Rivis'

*Crocus*

Forget-me-not (*Myosotis sylvatica*)

Granny's bonnet (*Aquilegia*)

Grape hyacinth (*Muscari*)

Hyacinth (*Hyacinthus*)

*Iris reticulata*

*Pulmonaria*

Rosemary (*Rosmarinus*)

*Scilla siberica*

### White

*Anemone*

*Camellia*

*Chaenomeles*

*Clematis armandii*

Crab apple (*Malus*)

*Crocus*

Daffodil (*Narcissus*)

Dog's tooth violet (*Erythronium*)

*Exochorda* x *macrantha* 'The Bride'

Foam flower (*Tiarella wherryi*)

Honeysuckle (*Lonicera fragrantissima*)

Hyacinth (*Hyacinthus*)

Japanese snowball bush (*Viburnum plicatum*)

*Leucojum* (Snowflake)

Lily-of-the-valley (*Convallaria majalis*)

*Magnolia*

Mexican orange blossom (*Choisya ternata*)

Ornamental cherry – blossom (*Prunus*)

Peony (*Paeonia*)

*Pulmonaria officinalis* 'Sissinghurst White'

*Skimmia japonica*

Tulip (*Tulipa*)

### Green

*Arum italicum* 'Pictum'

*Pulmonaria*

Spurge (*Euphorbia*)

## SUMMER

### Yellow

*Achillea*

*Anthemis*

*Bidens ferulifolia*

Black-eyed Susan (*Rudbeckia*)

*Canna*

Clematis

Coreopsis

Corydalis lutea

Dahlia

Daylily (Hemerocallis)

Evening primrose
(Oenothera)

Helenium

Honeysuckle (Lonicera)

Inula hookeri

Iris

Laburnum

Ligularia

Lily (Lilium)

Marguerite
(Argyranthemum)

Mullein (Verbascum)

Poppy (Papaver)

Potentilla

Robinia pseudoacacia
'Frisia'

Rose (Rosa)

Sunflower (Helianthus)

Zinnia

## Orange

Busy Lizzie (Impatiens)

Crocosmia

Dahlia

Daylily (Hemerocallis)

Geum

Helenium

Honeysuckle (Lonicera)

Lily (Lilium)

Marigold (Calendula,
Tagetes)

Nasturtium (Tropaeolum)

Potentilla

Red-hot poker (Kniphofia)

Rose (Rosa)

Spurge (Euphorbia
griffithii 'Fireglow')

Sunflower (Helianthus)

Zinnia

## Red

Bergamot (Monarda)

Canna

Clematis

Cosmos atrosanguineus

Crocosmia

Dahlia

Daylily (Hemerocallis)

Fuchsia

Geranium phaeum

Geum

Hollyhock (Alcea rosea)

Knautia macedonica

Lobelia

Lupin (Lupinus)

Lychnis coronaria

Nasturtium (Tropaeolum)

Pelargonium

Penstemon

Poppy (Papaver)

Potentilla

Red valerian (Centranthus
ruber)

Rose (Rosa)

Salvia

Zinnia

## Pink

Angel's fishing rod
(Dierama pulcherrimum)

Beauty bush (Kolkwitzia
amabilis)

Clematis

Cranesbill (Geranium)

Dahlia

Foxglove (Digitalis)

Lilac (Syringa)

Penstemon

Pink (Dianthus)

Poppy (Papaver)

Rhodochiton
atrosanguineus

Rock rose (Cistus)

Rose (Rosa)

Salvia

Spider flower (Cleome
hassleriana)

Sweet pea (Lathyrus)

## Blue

Agapanthus

Anchusa azurea 'Loddon
Royalist'

Blue flag (Iris versicolor)

Butterfly bush (Buddleja)

Campanula

Cider gum (Eucalyptus
gunnii)

Clematis

Corydalis flexuosa

Cranesbill (Geranium)

Delphinium

Hydrangea

Jacob's ladder
(Polemonium)

Lavender (Lavandula)

Lilac (Syringa)

Love-in-a-mist
(Nigella)

Meconopsis

Ornamental onion
(Allium)

**Pelargonium** 'Sunraysia'

Penstemon

Salvia

Sea holly (Eryngium)

Solanum crispum
'Glasnevin'

Sweet rocket (Hesperis
matronalis)

Verbena bonariensis

Viola

Wisteria

## White

Agapanthus

Artemesia 'Powis Castle'
– silver foliage

Baby's breath
(Gypsophila paniculata)

Bleeding heart (Dicentra
spectabilis alba)

Clematis

Cornus kousa

Crambe cordifolia

**Muscari latifolium**

Delphinium
Foxglove (*Digitalis*)
*Gaura lindheimeri*
*Geranium*
Golden feverfew
   (*Tanacetum*)
*Hydrangea*
*Iris laevigata*
Lavender (*Lavandula*)
*Leucanthemum*
Lilac (*Syringa*)
Lily (*Lilium*)
Loosestrife (*Lysimachia*)
*Lychnis coronaria* 'Alba'
Marguerite
   (*Argyranthemum*)
Mock orange
   (*Philadelphus*)
Ornamental onion
   (*Allium*)
*Osteospermum*
Rose (*Rosa*)

*Solanum jasminoides*
   'Album'
*Stachys byzantina* – silver
   foliage
Sweet rocket (*Hesperis*
   *matronalis*)
Tobacco plant (*Nicotiana*)
*Wisteria*

**Green**

*Agave*
*Alchemilla mollis*
*Angelica*
*Astilboides tabularis*
Banana (*Musa*)– foliage
*Brunnera macrophylla*
Buckler fern (*Dryopteris*)
*Canna* - foliage
Chinese rhubarb (*Rheum*
   *palmatum*)
*Darmera peltata*
Dogwood (*Cornus*)
Elder (*Sambucus*)
*Ensete ventricosum* –
   foliage
Feather grass (*Stipa*)
Feather reed grass
   (*Calamagrostis* x
   *acutiflora*)
Fennel (*Foeniculum*
   *vulgare*)
Fig (*Ficus*)
Grape vine (*Vitis*)
*Gunnera manicata*
Hair grass (*Deschampsia*)
*Hosta*
*Humulus lupulus* 'Aureus'
*Melianthus major*
*Miscanthus*

*Pennisetum*
Purple moor grass
   (*Molinia caerulea*)
*Ricinus communis* -
   foliage
*Rodgersia pinnata*
Sedge (*Carex*)

# AUTUMN
## Yellow

*Acer palmatum*\* – foliage
*Clematis tangutica*
*Cotoneaster* - berries
*Dahlia*
Firethorn (*Pyracantha*)
   – berries
Rowan (*Sorbus*) – berries
Witch hazel (*Hamamelis*)
   – foliage

## Orange

*Acer palmatum*\* – foliage
*Amelanchier* – foliage
*Berberis* – foliage
*Cercidiphyllum japonicum*
   – foliage
*Cotinus* – foliage
*Dahlia*
Dogwood (*Cornus*)
   – foliage
Grape vine (*Vitis*)
   – foliage
Firethorn (*Pyracantha*)
   – berries
*Fothergilla* – foliage
*Liquidambar* – foliage
*Nyssa sylvatica* – foliage
Ornamental cherry
   (*Prunus*) – foliage

*Physalis alkekengi* -
   berries
Red-hot poker (*Kniphofia*)
*Rhus typhina* – foliage
Rowan – berries (*Sorbus*)
Spindle tree (*Euonymus*)
   – foliage
Virginia creeper
   (*Parthenocissus*) –
   foliage

## Red

*Acer palmatum*\* – foliage
*Cercis canadensis* 'Forest
   Pansy'
*Cotoneaster* - berries
Crab apples (*Malus*) –
   berries
*Dahlia*
Firethorn (*Pyracantha*)
   – berries
*Fuchsia*
Kaffir lily (*Schizostyllis*
   *coccinea* 'Major')
Lords and ladies (*Arum*
   *italicum*) – berries
*Penstemon*
Rose (*Rosa*) – hips
Rowan (*Sorbus*) – berries
*Sedum*

## Pink

*Aster*
*Callicarpa bodinieri* var.
   *giraldi* - berries
*Colchicum*
*Cyclamen*
   *hederifolium*
*Dahlia*

Kaffir lily (*Schizostyllis coccinea* 'Jennifer')

*Nerine bowdenii*

**Blue**

*Aster*

*Gentiana**

Monkshood (*Aconitum*)

*Perovskia* 'Blue Spire'

*Salvia*

**White**

*Aster*

Christmas box (*Sarcococca humilis*)

*Crocus laevigatus*

*Gaura lindheimeri*

Japanese anemone (*Anemone* x *hybrida*)

Snowdrop (*Galanthus reginae-olgae*)

Strawberry tree (*Arbutus unedo*)

**Green**

See Winter Evergreen

# WINTER

**Yellow**

*Clematis cirrhosa*

Daffodil (*Narcissus* 'February Gold')

*Iris danfordiae*

*Mahonia*

*Phyllostachys vivax aureocaulis* - stems

Winter aconite (*Eranthis hyemalis*)

Winter jasmine (*Jasminum nudiflorum*)

Witch hazel (*Hamamelis*)

**Orange**

*Phyllostachys bambusoides* 'Allgold' - bamboo stems

**Red**

*Bergenia* 'Bressingham Salmon' - foliage

*Crocus tommasinianus* 'Ruby Giant'

Dogwood – stems (*Cornus alba* 'Sibirica')

*Iris foetidissima* (seeds)

Lenten rose (*Helleborus orientalis*)

*Parrotia persica*

*Prunus*

*Tilia platyphyllos* 'Rubra' - new red twigs

**Pink**

*Daphne mezereum*

*Viburnum* x *bodnantense*

**Blue**

*Iris reticulata*

*Iris unguicularis*

**White**

*Betula utilis* var. *jacquemontii* – bark

Christmas rose (*Helleborus niger* )

*Daphne bholua*

*Erica carnea* 'Golden Starlet'*

*Eucalyptus niphophila* – bark

Lenten rose (*Helleborus orientalis*)

*Rubus cockburnianus* – stems

Snowdrop (*Galanthus*)

*Viburnum tinus*

**Green**

*Helleborus argutifolius*

Lenten rose (*Helleborus orientalis*)

**Evergreen**

Box (*Buxus*)

*Camellia japonica*

Christmas box (*Sarcococca*)

Chusan palm (*Trachycarpus fortunei*)

*Cordyline australis*

*Cotoneaster*

Cypress (*Cupressus*)

*Daphne odora*

*Elaeagnus pungens*

*Eucalyptus*

*Euonymus fortunei*

False cypress (*Chamaecyparis*)

*Fatsia japonica*

*Garrya elliptica*

*Griselinia littoralis*

Heath (*Erica*)*

Heather (*Calluna*)*

*Hebe*

Holly (*Ilex*)

Ivy (*Hedera*)

*Itea ilicifolia*

Juniper (*Juniperus*)

Lavender (*Lavandula*)

Loquat (*Eriobotrya japonica*)

*Magnolia grandiflora*

*Mahonia*

Mexican orange blossom (*Choisya ternata*)

*Osmanthus*

Pine (*Pinus*)

Portugal laurel (*Prunus lusitanica*)

Privet (*Ligustrum*)

Rosemary (*Rosmarinus*)

Silver fir (*Abies*)

*Skimmia*

Spruce (*Picea*)

*Thuja*

Thyme (*Thymus*)

*Viburnum davidii*

*Vinca*

Yew (*Taxus*)

***Dahlia* 'Ellen Huston'**

## PICTURE ACKNOWLEDGMENTS

All photographs copyright Anness Publishing
Limited with the exception of the following
pages: 3, 16r, 18cr, 19cr, 19br, 20l, 21r,
22, 24br, 25cl, 25c, 46, 70t, 71, 77l, 77r,
80l, 84l, 84r, 85 © Jonathan Buckley.